HOW TO HEAL YOUR SOUL

Your Path to Peace of Mind

Anthony Glenn

TABLE OF CONTENTS

Do you feel like something is missing, even though you feel as though you have everything and should be happy?

You are not alone. There are thousands of people all over the world waking up every morning feeling empty. They fall asleep in the evening asking themselves, "Is that all? Is this everything life has to give? Why am I not happy? What is wrong with me?"

Nothing is wrong with you. Your soul is suffering. That is what is wrong. Your soul needs you, your attention, and to find a supportive friend in you.

This book is here to help you heal. It is like a friend who understands you but that also has the answers. This friend knows what should you do and exactly how things will become better.

So, if you want to find inner peace and heal your soul, listen to what this book has to say. Then, pick out some of the advice that best suits you and let it inspire you to begin your healing journey.

INTRODUCTION

Understand Your Soul

The True Nature of a Soul

Since the very beginning of the world, people have been asking about the true nature of a soul. Is it just a breath? Could it really be measured and found to weigh 21 grams? Or is it all nonsense because our soul is much, much more than that? What about our splendid ideas, everlasting love, and unbearable pain? All of that can fit into 21 grams of air? Not nearly.

In our world, centered about reason, logic, and physical reality, the concept of a soul is pretty marginalized. Science has no explanation for this because there is still no adequate system to examine it. So, they do not say that souls do not exist, because we all know that is not true. But they leave what it is up to you to conclude or believe. All of the world's religions have their explanation of the real nature of souls, but for many people out there these concepts are not enough.

So, it seems to be up to oneself to come to a conclusion about souls and to choose what to believe.

We know that we have a body, a mind, and a third thing, which is sometimes called a soul and sometimes a spirit. This third component is what we will talk about. For balance, you need all three parts to be healthy and to work properly. The soul and the spirit are actually two sides of the same thing: our non-physical side.

The soul represents the feminine side of us while the spirit is the masculine component of our non-physical selves. Our emotions, imagination, passion, desires, and creativity are matters of our feminine energy. On the other side, our masculine energy is comprised of intellect, willpower, action, motivation, and productivity. For the wellbeing of your soul, it is crucial to appreciate and nourish your feminine energy.

The Divine in Every Human

Regardless of your religion, you should agree we all have something divine in us. That sparkle is what we are talking about, our soul. It is our higher self, a special place where all of our great ideas and wonderful emotions come from. We all have this. We all have some stardust within ourselves. And through that higher part, we are connected with the Divine. It does not matter what your religion is or which god you believe in. This is a spiritual relationship. Spirituality is not the same as religion. It is a private, personal relationship with the Divine. Everybody has that relationship. It may be excellent or dysfunctional (if you are an atheist, for example), but you certainly have it.

You are not your body. You are not your mind, intellect, or thoughts. You are not just a spirit. You are all of that together and something more. For a balanced wholeness, it is essential to take care of each of these parts.

Emotions are the Soul Speaking

Your soul is here and it needs to communicate with you. But we often do not hear it because it is quieter than the concerns of everyday life. It does not scream like an unpaid bill or our family if we ignore it. Your soul is trying to talk to you through your emotions. If you do not recognize it and do nothing, it will become a bit louder. If you still do not pay attention, your soul will suffer and will try a few more times to warn you. If you still do not recognize it, it will send you other, more apparent signals like illnesses or injuries. It is wiser to acknowledge that emotions are the language of the soul than to wait for everything in your life to break so that you can hear it. So, listen to what your soul is saying. Maybe it has something important to tell you.

WHEN THE SOUL
IS SUFFERING

We all know very well when something is wrong with our body. It has its own systems such as physical pain to make this obvious and to force us to pay attention.
But with the soul, things are different. It is quieter and does not scream for attention. Besides that, we are taught not to be too emotional and to focus more on solving practical problems.

Neglecting the soul is also common in this materialistic and logic-oriented world. This is a massive problem because nourishing our souls is crucial for happiness. While chasing other external things that we think will make us happy, we forget to pay attention to this essential element in ourselves. While we rush from one task to another, to achieve one more goal and to become more of one thing or another, our soul is starving. It does not get its much-needed love, attention, nourishment, understanding, and support. It is crying inside while we are asking why we are not happy when we have everything, saying "What is wrong with me? What is wrong with my achievements?"

Well, maybe by reading this you are moving in the right direction. Perhaps the problem is not in your education, your spouse, or your beautiful house. It is not even in the event that you are blaming: the end of a relationship, a loss, an illness, etc. Unhappiness is an inside problem. It is about your soul. If you see yourself in the following examples and this all sounds too familiar, it may be time for some soul healing.

1. You do not feel joy and you find it hard to be present and enjoy the moment.
Wherever you look, you can see only more and more obligations. It is hard for you to relax and be here and now. Your mind is continuously jumping to the past or the future, and nothing brings you pure joy.

2. You lack enthusiasm or motivation.
Your enthusiasm has faded away and you are no longer excited about new projects or a new day. Your "why" is not strong enough to make you move.

3. You have lost your playfulness and laughter.
You simply do not know how to play and laugh without expectations anymore, without pressure and just for joy. You have convinced yourself that you do not have time to waste on play or fun.

4. You feel fatigue and want to escape.
All you need is a pause in your life, to take a rest from everything, everyone, your daily life, and yourself. You feel enough.

5. You feel like you lack a purpose and a meaning for life.
Maybe you have not found your purpose, but you believe that it must exist. You need to seek it again. But when your soul is hurt, nothing has enough meaning.

6. You feel stuck.
Our vital energy, like every other kind of energy, does not like to be still. It must flow. When the soul feels stuck, everything is blocked. You cannot move forward without solving what is bothering your soul.

7. You find it hard to be a good friend.

Perhaps you are a good friend in general, but you have been finding it hard to be there for the people that are dear to you for some time. You cannot share in their happiness and do not have enough compassion or empathy for their feelings.

8. You are depressed, anxious, or are having panic attacks.

If you have any of these psychological issues - or any others - your soul is undoubtedly suffering. It is time for a big soul cleaning and some serious work on yourself.

9. You have some eating problems such as overeating, anorexia, or bulimia.

What are you trying to do, eat the problem? Or are you trying to starve your body like your soul? Food is the fuel for our energy. You need to find the balance.

10. You do not sleep well.

Sleep is the time to recharge our energy, to find peace, and to rest our bodies and minds. If your soul is suffering, it will try to reach you when you are in silence so that you can hear it. That is why you may have sleeping issues. The best thing to do is to listen to what your soul is telling you.

11. Your behavior is either destructive or self-destructive.

If you are doing more harm than good to others or yourself, this is another sign that your soul needs attention. This cannot be your true nature.

12. You have an addiction problem.

Maybe you are trying to find an instant fix and to avoid an unpleasant conversation with your soul. That leads exactly nowhere.

13. You became a workaholic.

You are trying to hide from yourself behind a mountain of work. Being busy is not the solution. Your soul is still within you, waiting for you to pause. If you do not do so, it will make you ill to force you to stop.

14. Your relationships suffer.

If your most important relationship - the one you have with yourself - is suffering, none of the relationships in your life can work well. The healing must begin with you.

15. You get sick or injured.

As we already mentioned, if you stubbornly avoid hearing the voice of your soul, it will become louder. If you still do not hear it, it will warn you. But if you still do not react, it will hit you with a big problem that you cannot ignore.

16. You feel like something is wrong, but cannot explain what exactly.

People often think that something is wrong with them because they know that something is missing, but they do not have a name for it. That still does not mean that everything is fine or that you should pretend it is. It would be weird to go to your physician and tell him, "Doctor, my soul is suffering." But there are many people out there whose job it is to cure the soul. These include psychologists, psychiatrists, and coaches as well as the numerous self-help books and podcasts which can be your pathway to wholeness.

WHY DOES THIS HAPPEN?

Possible Reasons for the Suffering of the Soul

Maybe you know exactly what in your life is not going as you wish and what would make you happy. But many people do not know for sure what is missing or why they feel that something is wrong even though everything looks perfect from the outside.

In general, our soul is suffering if it is hurt, not treated well, not nourished, or not taken care of. A neglected, underestimated, and starved soul must suffer.

Here are some typical cases where your soul may be suffering.

- Carrying the past with yourself, refusing to leave it behind or to let it go.
You have to leave the past behind so that you can enjoy the present. This is the only real time and the only reality where you can be happy. If your soul is still in pain from past experiences, you need to dig them up and reframe them. It is time to get clear with yourself what have you learn from the previous lessons and let them go with gratefulness and love, so you could move on and heal your soul.

- Unhappy upbringing, traumas from childhood.
They say it is never too late for a happy childhood. That is because as an adult you have the ability to cure the fears from your early years. Now you have the power to understand the circumstances and the people who hurt you, their intentions, and their emotions. You are not that child anymore. You are a

stable adult who can offer support to your inner child.

- Painful events such as the end of a relationship, loss, or illness. Those are challenging situations from which the soul needs some help and time to recover. That is why we will talk about these cases later.

- Emotional suppression.
If you ignore unpleasant emotions, that is the same as hiding them under the carpet. After some time, there will be a hill of clutter and you will fall over it.

- Constantly running to achieve goals and to chase happiness.
This may come as a surprise, but if you are focused only on a goal, instead of enjoying the process, that will not make you happy. On the contrary, you will miss out on many moments which could nourish your soul and will overlook many things that you could be thankful for. Rushing towards a goal makes you stressed and prevents you from finding your inner peace.

THE IMPACT OF SOUL SUFFERING ON OTHER LIFE AREAS

When the soul does not feel good, everything suffers. It affects all areas of our lives: our health, families, relationships, and work.

Our wholeness includes our bodies, minds, and souls. Only if all three of these are well can we say that we are healthy. There is no health without any one of these. Too often, we only take care of our bodies. Our minds usually get some attention through education because society appreciates intellect. Mental health is another story. It is not a priority until something goes wrong, but many of us know that we need to develop our minds.

But the soul is too often neglected. This goes so far that many of us are not even aware of its presence and do not care about its needs. We tend to think that what our soul is asking for is not important, that this is a luxury for those with too much money and spare time.

When does this change? There are two possible options. The first one is a blessing - if you wake up while it is not too late. You become aware of how crucial it is for your wellbeing to satisfy the needs of your soul. Then you can reconnect with your deepest self, work on your spirituality, and your life will receive an incredible turnover.

The second option is not as sweet as the first one, but is, unfortunately, more common. The waking up and the turnover come later after something has already gone wrong. You fall ill or get injured and that forces you to stop and look into yourself.

If it is not too serious, you are lucky. But if you have ignored the signs for a long time, this can be your last chance to wake up. Then you will have to deal with the panic, too. There are lots of books written about the connection between our health, minds, and souls. For us, it is important to know that every illness is just a symptom that means that something inside of us is not as it should be. Classic medicine can cure those symptoms but it overlooks the actual problem which is much broader. It is a toxic emotion. We will talk further about this kind of feeling, but for now, you should be aware that is a poison which is literally killing you. What is hidden behind a sour emotion? Some thought or belief which is working against us while our suffering soul is screaming for help.

If you have any health issues, from the flu or a cold to a broken arm or cancer, remember that this is the symptom of a deeper problem. This can be both good and bad news. It can be scary to admit that you have neglected yourself. But it is also good to know that you have the power within yourself to heal and recover. It will indeed be a hard job, but you need to dive deep into yourself and reconnect with your true nature.

If your soul is malnourished and painful, you will not be able to recharge. So you will lack energy and will not have much to give or to put into anything. Besides your damaged health, your relationships will suffer. We cannot take care of anyone else if we are not okay ourselves. We cannot be good parents, good partners, good sons or daughters, or even good pet owners if we are falling apart on the inside. Nobody wants a yelling, stressed mom or an emotionally distant dad. To fix our relationship with others, we need to heal ourselves first.

Your job will also suffer, no matter how much you used to love what you did in the first place. If you lose your motivation and enthusiasm, you will miss out on the passion and your productivity will be lower. So something that was your beloved career may turn into simply finishing dull tasks to pay the bills while you cannot wait for the end of the workday to arrive.

It is obvious how harmful this can it be to everything in your life. You can neither give your best in anything nor live your life to the fullest.

Now you are aware of how dangerous it can be to carry around a bleeding soul. It is a crucial problem that yearns to be solved. Do not ignore it. Invest some time into understanding and recovering your relationship with your inner self.

TOXIC FEELINGS

Emotions are the voice of our soul. It is crucial to hear and understand them so that you can stay connected with or even reconnect with your inner self. But, we all know that there are some rough feelings. What about them? What are they telling us? How can we cope with them?

It is perfectly normal to experience negative feelings. Imagine your emotions as navigation. The positive ones tell you that you are on the right path while the negative ones say that you are going in the wrong direction. It would be stupid to hate or avoid someone only because they are warning you that you are doing something wrong. The same thing happens with our bitter feelings. You need to understand what the emotion is telling you, accept it, and do something about it. Then the irritating voice saying, "Turn left. Turn left!" will disappear.

But, it is an entirely different story with constant negative feelings. If you constantly feel low, that will affect all areas of your life. These kinds of emotions are toxic and are poisoning your life. It is like you have an enemy within yourself. Carrying this baggage acidifies your life and causes self-sabotage.

Concerning your energy, these toxic feelings mean that you have huge pools of toxic energy within. If you do not take any action regarding them, they can drain the vitality from your life. Chronic toxic emotions make you predisposed to repeat the cycle of negative experiences and never reach your full potential.

Which Emotions are Toxic?

It is normal to sometimes experience anger, rational fear, or sadness. It is not okay, however, to dive deep into those feelings and stay there forever. So, let us find out what is poisoning your soul from the inside. Each of the following emotions is toxic if it is chronic:

- Anxiety
- General fear
- Anger
- Guilt
- Shame
- Sadness
- Regret
- Chronic discomfort
- Chronic dissatisfaction
- Self-loathing
- Bitterness
- Resentment
- Addiction
- Envy
- Jealousy
- Frustration
- Depression

So, if you have recognized some or even all of these in yourself, what can you do about them? The first step is becoming aware of your feelings. Acknowledge that they are there and accept them. Admit to yourself what you really feel, without judgment. You would not like to talk about your emotions with someone who is judging you, right? Be a good friend to yourself and listen without validating. For example, you could say, "Okay, I'm jealous. Now I am aware of it."

"Why do I feel like this?" is the next question you need to ask yourself. Try to understand the reason why you feel the way you do. What is at the root of this feeling? What am I trying to tell others by feeling and acting like this? What is hidden behind this emotion? What belief of mine is provoking it?

The next step is action. It begins with the question, "What can I do about this?" You need to search for more constructive ways to respond to situations in your life. In short, you need to replace those toxic feelings with positive and nurturing ones. There are many techniques which can help you do that. The basic mechanism behind them is pretty simple: to change your emotions, you need to change the thoughts that provoke them. So, you need to maintain a positive mindset and put some effort into working on your beliefs. And things will change, starting with your feelings. Your soul will be healed with no more enemies to break the peace from the inside.

We will give you some examples of the general direction you should think about certain negative emotions.

If you constantly feel anxious, are overwhelmed by fear, discouraged, or have problems with concentration or sleep, it is as if you are seeking a solution to a problem all the time - just without the solution. This is not constructive at all and often is pretty irrational. Think about why you feel like that. What makes you feel insecure and threatened? What are you afraid of? There must be a fear behind it. What do you believe? What is so scary about that scenario? And why do you think you are not able to take it? Once you find your answers, look at which of them are irrational. Replace them with better ones. For example, tell yourself, "I can take whatever life brings me." Try to face your fears and find the difference between reality and your thoughts. Do your best to get control over your mind. The easiest way to do this is to start meditating. That way, you will learn how to direct your thoughts the way you want. Learn to relax your whole body and breathe deeply. Make physical exercising your routine and surround yourself with people who think positively.

Toxic Anger

If it is well-managed and happens from time to time with a real reason, anger can be healthy and can help you solve some problems. But if it is your pattern and you find yourself angry too often, it is time to do something about it. What is behind your anger? Do you feel hurt or insecure? What message are you trying to send to those around you by acting like that? If you slow down, look deep into yourself, and start working on your mindfulness, you will be able to take full responsibility for your happiness and will act from a different place, the place of inner peace. Your toxic anger will melt like a snowflake and it will be much nicer for others to be around you and for you to be around yourself, too.

Do you often blame yourself for different things and feel guilty for things you cannot control? Do you ever find yourself feeling responsible for other's feelings? It is important to find the difference between taking responsibility for your life, your happiness, your decisions, and your choices on the one side and your guilt on the other. Taking responsibility is a must and is the first step towards personal growth. Feeling guilty is not constructive at all. It drains you and makes you feel terrible.

It is also essential to differentiate actual guilt from toxic guilt. If you do something bad and violate the law intentionally, of course, you are guilty. Like it or not, that is not toxic, and you need a lawyer, not a coach. If you do something wrong, say you are sorry, explain your actions, and ask for forgiveness. Learn from your mistakes and do not repeat them.

21

But, if you feel guilty when someone around you is feeling bad, this is a sign that you still carry some emotional baggage from childhood. You probably felt responsible for the happiness of your parents and felt guilty when they had problems. Perhaps no one explained that it was not about you. Talk to the child that you were, hug them mentally, and teach them that everybody is responsible for their own happiness. The only things you are responsible for are your happiness, your choices, your decisions, your behavior, your body, your mind, your words, your children, your pets, and your belongings. You should be kind and make others happy whenever you can. But you did not come to this world to only make others happy. Everybody has to do so for themselves. Do not take the responsibility for and feel guilty about things that you cannot control.

Shame is one more emotion that comes from a very low vibration. The fundamental belief behind it is "I'm not good enough." The other basic thing behind it is a fear of being abandoned. Embarrassment often prevents us from fulfilling our dreams, and we miss out on opportunities to enjoy ourselves because of the fear of looking ridiculous.

If this is your kind of poison, you will need a lot of self-love. Why do you think you are not good enough? What should you be to feel that you are acceptable? Why is the judgment of others so important to you? Is it really so important what someone would think about what you are doing? Who are those insecure people who judge you? Is their opinion relevant to you? Set yourself free from the boundaries which are not yours. People who love you will still love you and those who do not... well, they will always find a reason, no matter what you do. And remember: you are enough. You are smart enough, tall enough, rich enough, talkative enough, whatever-you-worry-about enough. You are good enough.

Sadness is also a perfectly normal emotion to have when you experience a loss or a tragedy. Give yourself some time to work through it. Do not try to suppress that feeling because it will hit you much stronger later, like a boomerang. But if you stay stuck in this state for too long, your life may stagnate. It will come to the point where you have to move on. If you refuse to do so, that may lead to bigger problems and depression. So, what can you do to be able to move on? Let it go. Let the past stay in the past. Accept it, get over it, and let it go. Forgive everything you have to forgive and everyone who needs your forgiveness. That way you will set yourself free. We are not saying that you need to agree with someone who hurt you. Just give yourself the gift of forgiveness. Permit yourself to let it go and get rid of that heavy baggage. If you have experienced the grief of a loss, try to recall all of the good memories and be grateful for them. Be thankful for having such a person in your life. Hug them in your thoughts, say thank you, and let them go. After these mental and spiritual exercises, you will be free to make plans for a bright future.

Chronic discomfort and dissatisfaction become toxic when they are permanent. It is okay to feel discomfort from time to time, this may mean that you are leaving your comfort zone and growing as a person. Dissatisfaction can force you to search for new solutions and become better each day. It is okay to be ambitious and strive forward. But if you are never satisfied, that is toxic perfectionism. You need to accept yourself and your imperfect human nature. Constant discomfort produces more stress than good, so try to slow down and rest in your comfort zone regularly.

Bitterness usually goes hand in hand with resentment and a feeling of injustice. It is a mature form of anger and a mask behind which is always hidden a hurt soul. Maybe you were poorly treated as a child, bullied, ignored, or some injustices were done to you. Or you experienced the pain of grief which you never got over. Anyway, you were probably bitter for many years. Very few bitter people get the help they need to understand of others. This is not surprising considering the nature of the problem. But, what a bitter person really needs is support and help to recognize their problem and then to go in the direction which will melt it down. So, if your soul's poison has this bitter taste, you need to admit that you have a problem. You were probably hurt in the past and then developed this attitude. But it is not constructive. It does not serve your higher good. You need to let go of all the anger, bitterness, and resentment, to accept your old pain, and shed some tears over it. Then you will be free to experience the life full of possibilities that you deserve.

Envy and jealousy - well, these feelings can hardly be called healthy. Behind them is usually the hidden belief that there is not enough for everyone. Maybe you grew up in a low-income family where there was not enough money, room, food, or things for everybody. Or you grew up with a large family with many siblings and a constant feeling that there was not enough parental love for everyone. Do you often feel that if someone is rich, that makes you poor? That you are the one who deserves their money and it is something that should belong to you, not the other? These beliefs are limiting and do not do you any good. The universe is full of everything. There is enough for everyone - enough money, love, happiness, health, enough of everything you need or want. Even though some people tend to accept jealousy as a sign of love, it has hardly anything to do with true love. It only shows a lack of self-confidence and insecurity. That is why it is so crucial to grow self-love and build a mature relationship with yourself first, before a relationship with another person. The cure, again, is to look inside yourself, not in trying to control others.

Addiction is one more sign of a pained soul. We try to compensate and find in an outside person or thing what is missing inside ourselves. If you "cannot live without" your spouse, phone, sweets, drugs, alcohol, cigarettes, or anything else, it poisons your life.

If you expect the other person to be responsible for your happiness, that is not a mature, healthy relationship. You should both be whole people who love to be together. That is all. It can sound romantic when someone cannot live without you, but leave that for poems and novels. In real life, you should be able to live well with or without them. Otherwise, it becomes pretty hard to survive before the happily ever after.

If you are constantly hiding behind a curtain of smoke, ask yourself what you are hiding from. If you have the habit of visiting bars and trying to drown your sadness in alcohol or to take drugs to escape reality, what are you running from? These solutions only make problems worse. Start by becoming aware of your addiction. Take responsibility and then take steps to heal from the inside.

Handling frustrations is a part of being an adult. We all feel frustrated from time to time. But it should not become chronic. If you do nothing about it, that will make you feel helpless, which is the path to depression. And if it becomes chronic, depression itself is very close to rock bottom. It is not impossible to return from there, but you will need to put a lot of effort into soul healing.

How to Heal Your Soul and Find Peace

Make Spirituality a Priority

Did you take a shower today? Did you brush your teeth? "Of course," you think, "what is the purpose behind these silly questions?" And what did you do for your mental hygiene today? Do you practice meditation, gratefulness, prayer, visualization, and affirmations on a daily basis? Or do you do some other things which make you happy like yoga, some other sport, reading, writing, drawing, or any other hobby? How do you nourish your soul? If you do nothing about it - do not feed it, do not clean it, do not recharge your positive energy - how do you expect it to be alright? Why is it awkward not to take care of your personal hygiene, but you find it shameful to take care of your mental hygiene?

You find it normal to fuel your car, recharge your phone battery, and probably also to nourish your body with proper food, but you forget to recharge your own energy.

You know you have to feed your pet, but forget to nurture your own soul. You do not skip washing the dishes, but cannot find time to clean and polish your beliefs. Then, afterward, you ask why you feel hurt, neglected, and miserable. That is not a secret at all. If you do not clean and tidy your home, you will live in a dirty mess. If you do not practice mental hygiene on a daily basis, you will have clutter in your mind and soul.

Positivity must be exercised like our muscles. No one is surprised if they lose strength after not visiting the gym for a while. Why, then, is it so hard to accept that positivity also requires some work from us?

There are three common reasons among people who do not work on their self-growth.

Reason #3
I'm suspicious that will have an effect.

If this is your reason for not taking any action towards your inner space, you have three possible options to solve it.

You can read, become informed, gain some theoretical knowledge, and learn about other's experiences with this from literature.

The second option is to observe real examples either around you or on the internet. You can view their experiences, their actions, their transformations, and their results.

And the third, most effective way, is to give it a try. Suspicious people want to examine everything and then come to a conclusion. This is the best of all possible ways. Try to apply the bits of advice that you like and watch what happens. Along the way your doubts will melt, and, incidentally, your soul will enjoy itself.

If you still do not want to give it a try, then the reason is not that you are suspicious. You just do not feel it is true or right for you.

Reason #2
I do not know how to become more spiritual, practice mindfulness, and begin self-growth.

This is the simplest reason you can have but also the most banal one. We live in the era of the internet where all of the world's knowledge is available to everyone. Everything you need to know to begin your self-growth journey and the process of healing your soul is just one click away. So, do not hide behind this reason. There is no excuse for not learning what you want to know. And not wanting to know is another thing.

And the **#1 most common reason** loved by people who do not take action is: *I do not have time for that.*

This one is the favorite of most. And it is a complete lie. It is as if you see the red light which signals that you ran out of fuel but move on because you do not want to waste your time stopping at a gas station. The truth may surprise you, but you have time for everything that is important to you. It is a matter of priorities. If something is important enough, you will make time for it. That is all. If you have enough time in your day to check social networks, to read the news, or to watch TV, you have enough time to work on yourself. The key is to make your spirituality and self-growth a priority. Think about your goals, the life you want, and how would you feel if you had inner peace. Then reserve some time every day for a new routine.

Change Your Point of View

Imagine one person that you cannot stand, someone who hurt you and who you do not want to see ever again. Imagine that person coming into the room where you are. There is one more person with you who do not know the other. You can predict what would you think and feel about that meeting. But what about that other person who does not know anything about your relationship? What would they think about the visitor? Would they have negative thoughts and feel anger or pain? Hardly. The difference between the two of you is your point of view. It is not about the other person. It is about your thoughts. You can notice the same thing in cases when something happens and someone is happy and satisfied, while someone else is sad and disappointed. There is the same event, but different points of view, again.

Why is the point of view important? Because that determines your thoughts which provoke your feelings. So, your overall happiness depends on the point of view you choose.

What can you do about it?

There will always be some situations that we can do nothing about. You cannot control everything. But what you can choose is your attitude. You can choose to look through the eyes of love and understanding or through hateful and judgmental ones. The reality would be the same in both cases, but you will feel differently. So why would anyone choose to be unhappy and stuck when they could live their dream life instead?

If you choose to adopt a positive mindset, besides all of the good effects you will experience, your point of view will give you more joy and you will live a happier life. That is a pretty good reason for choosing your point of view carefully, right?

People tend to notice the negative aspects of everything and think it is a consequence of their superior intelligence. We are taught to believe that negative thinking is more realistic than positive thinking. But that is completely untrue. Positive outcomes and events have the same odds of happening as negative ones. But thinking positively has far more chances to make you happy than thinking negatively. It may look superficial to some, but do not hesitate to search for something good in everything.

How to Be Introspective

You cannot work on something if you are not aware of it. If you want to change your life and heal your soul, you need to work on your thoughts, beliefs, and emotions. So, you have to dive deep into yourself to re-examine your beliefs, to become aware of your thoughts and patterns, and to find the roots of your feelings. Some pretty serious work is waiting for you. The most basic thing you have to do is to look into yourself. This is what we call introspection. It must be done at the very beginning of any self-growth journey or soul healing process.

You can practice introspection every day as a part of your daily routine or whenever you feel the need for it. Whenever something is bothering you, turn to yourself first and look inside for the reason. *What do I feel this way? Where this emotion is coming from? Which thought provoked me into feeling this way? What belief is hidden behind it?* Continue on in this way until everything is clear. It is best to practice introspection in silence, alone, without any distractions. Prepare yourself in advance and make plans about when you will do it. Sit in silence. It is best to begin by calming down, focusing on your breath. You can turn on some calming music or burn a candle to make a more peaceful atmosphere which will help you to relax.

If you decide to practice meditation as well, it is a good idea to combine these two activities as meditating first will help you come to more clear conclusions during introspection. It is also good to have a piece of paper and a pen to write down your thoughts and feelings. That way it will be easier to track your stream of thoughts and to not forget what came to you. It is also helpful to have it all written down just in case you want to go through it again.

Be patient with yourself and do not be disappointed if you do not come to some spectacular "Ah ha!" moments the few first times. They will come later when you become more mindful and present. After some practice, it will become a routine. You will constantly be introspective, not only as a ritual, but many times during the day, and will be constantly aware of all the processes happening in your mind and soul.

How to Love Yourself

What does this mean? And how could you possibly not love yourself? This may sound awkward at first, but we often do not love ourselves enough. You show a lack of love for yourself when you are shy, underestimate yourself, do not stand up for yourself, beat yourself up mentally, or grow toxic thoughts and feelings until your body gets sick. Some authors and therapists say that all problems in our lives and all of our health issues come from a lack of self-love.

How do we arrive at that point? We are all born as perfect babies, full of pure love, in harmony with ourselves and the world. What happens to those angels to allow them to become self-loathing grownups with no love for themselves? Growing up happens as do the adults around us. We learn about ourselves, life, and the world from them. We learn from what they tell us, how they treat us, and from their behavior. We subconsciously accept their patterns and beliefs and move far from our true nature. We believe we are not worthy and that we do not deserve love. This is how we begin to starve our souls.

So, if you want to reverse the process and stop being your inner enemy, you need to start loving yourself again.

How can you do that?

The things you have heard many times and perhaps believed to be true in some situations makes up everything you believe about yourself. What do you believe about yourself? What do you think is wrong with you? Why are you not enough? Why do you not deserve all the best the life has to give? What did you listen to while growing up?

Give yourself enough time to dig through all of these things. It may be painful, but those things have to be brought out into the sunlight. When you become aware and understand where all of this came from, you will be able to exchange them for more loving and supportive beliefs.

In the beginning, try to look into your own eyes in the mirror and tell yourself, "I love you." It may be weird, but you should hear it from yourself.

Repeat the following: "I love myself. I accept myself. I'm worthy. I deserve love and happiness." Repeat those affirmations until they become your new beliefs.

Be kind to yourself and try to make choices which will work towards your highest good. Do not hesitate to take actions which could make you happy.

Loving yourself does not mean just going to the spa or eating your favorite cake. It means pushing yourself in the direction you know is the right one. It means you have to force yourself to do what is best for you.

How to Practice Meditation for Soul Healing

If your soul is suffering, the primary reason is that you are disconnected from it. To start healing, you have to reconnect with your deepest self. Too often there are too many things standing in the way to hear the voice of your soul. All the hustle of everyday life, the constant rush, and the long to-do lists make you ignore the needs of your soul. The best thing you can do to hear it is to slow down and silence your mind.

There is no better way to do so than with meditation.

How to begin meditation?

It is a pretty simple yet powerful practice. Everything you need, you already have. Find a silent place, sit alone, and focus on your breathing. You can sit on the floor or in a chair, but with the right posture. You should be comfortable, but not too cozy - you do not want to fall asleep during meditation.

The goal is to achieve a complete presence in the moment, with awareness of everything inside and around yourself. In the absence of thought, when your mind is calm, you can get in touch with your inner self and clearly hear the voice of your soul.

Just sit still and focus on your breath. You can count inhales and exhales. When some thoughts come (as they inevitably will), just notice them and let them go. Repeat this every time a thought arises and practice staying focused on your breathing. It will become more comfortable with time and practice.

Do not think about the meditation affects you are hoping for. Just be fully present and let your higher self find the best way to guide you and reveal everything you need to heal your soul.

How Can a Healthy Lifestyle Help You Heal Your Soul?

Your body is the temple of your soul. You need to take care of it and keep it in good condition if you wish for your soul to feel comfortable inside.

What is the best way to take care of your body?

Choose a healthy lifestyle. This means sleeping and resting enough, eating the right amount of healthy food, as well as exercising and moving enough in ways that give you pleasure. It may be challenging to incorporate all of these changes into your busy lifestyle, but your body will thank you. You will experience many benefits from putting some effort into adopting new habits.

Start with what is the easiest for you. Sleep a bit more, start exercising, or make a healthy change in your eating habits.

When it comes to sleeping, only a couple of hours can make a huge difference. And it would be best if those additional hours were before midnight. That way, thanks to hormones, you will gain the best recovery and recharging of your body and mind. In the beginning, try to go to sleep an hour earlier than usual. Later, you may find that you like to wake up earlier and have some spare time for yourself. Try to sleep in complete darkness and silence. Choose the proper mattress and pillows, set a lower temperature in the room, and enjoy at least eight hours of quality, uninterrupted sleep. When you are well-rested, the sun shines brighter and everything is much easier. So do not overlook this critical factor for life satisfaction.

Another of those three crucial parts of your wellbeing is food. The right diet is the same as the right fuel for an engine. Stop unhealthy habits such as consuming fast food, sugar, white flour, soda, overeating, or undereating if you practice the opposite approach. Try to eat balanced, correctly-sized meals that are rich in quality nutrients. Add more fresh fruit and vegetables to your menu and drink a lot of water. The average adult needs about eight glasses of water per day to stay well hydrated. You can consult a nutritionist for a personalized menu to support the right diet just for you. Another option is to get informed about healthy food and then do your best to apply it to your daily routine.

Exercising is the most challenging change for many people. We are naturally predisposed to move, not to have a sedentary lifestyle. Begin with a short walk or an easy workout for about ten minutes each day to form a habit. Then you can prolong your exercise time, include some harder training, or begin doing the sports activity which you enjoy most.

It has been proven both scientifically and by experience that proper sleep, the correct nutrition, and exercise are the basis for a balanced life. This can cure a large part of mental issues and negative emotions such as anxiety, fear, sleeping problems, depression, and so on.

These are three crucial steps you need to take to change your lifestyle into a healthy one. Whatever you choose to begin with, be patient and persistent. Every behavior needs at least 21 days to become a habit.

Soul Food

We all know that we have to nourish our bodies on a daily basis. If we skip a meal, our stomach becomes noisy and painful to remind us of that fact.

But our soul is much quieter. If we forget to nurture it for a while, it will patiently wait for us to remember and to pay attention to it. But do not think that your soul is not suffering in the meantime. It is starving without food. What is the food of the soul? Everything which makes you happy and which makes you feel alive. Everything which makes your life worth living. Everything which gives you pleasure. This may be art, literature, music, friendship, hobbies, nature, gardening, or anything else that you really enjoy.

If you still do not know what makes you happy, we have collected some suggestions of activities that science says can have an impact on one's level of happiness.

Grow Your Relationships

Socializing is a significant factor in our happiness. People who grow their relationships with friends and family are more satisfied overall. So, stay in touch with your friends even if you are not able to see each other very often. Surround yourself with people who have a positive mindset and are pleasant company. The process of soul healing is easier if you have someone to talk to.

Use Your Creativity and Imagination

Running away from your problems is never a good idea. Escaping by using your imagination is also not a practical option. But using your imagination and creativity can work miracles for the quality of your life and your healing. Ask the child in yourself what it would enjoy the most. What did you like to do as a child? Drawing, painting, coloring, crafts, playing an instrument, dancing? Recall what made you happy as a kid. Why will not you do that now as an adult? You can try out many options before picking the right one. Get some paper, crayons, coloring books, and stickers then have some fun. Playing is not just for kids. Playing is a part of human nature. Heal your life through music, dance, art - whatever makes you smile.

Carefully choose what you input into your mind and soul. Avoid negative news, activities, company, and anything that drains you. Choose nourishing books, movies, people, supportive ideas, and positive approaches to life. Give your soul plenty of quality food so that it has enough energy for healing and growth.

Spend some time in nature. As it is healthy for our lungs and a pleasure for our eyes, it is also a spa for our mind and a cure for our soul.

PUTTING THE PAST BEHIND YOU, LETTING GO, AND FORGIVING

To live your dream life, be happy, and have a joyful soul, you have to learn how to leave the past where it belongs: in the past. As long as you hold on to something and refuse to let it go, it will follow you wherever you go. No matter how bright your future could be, you will always carry around that heavy baggage. It is hard to fly when you are carrying a suitcase, rucksack, bag, and a huge melon with yourself. So, it is time to let go. It is time to set aside that heavy ballast of painful experiences, sadness, regret, and disappointment.

Look at your past as a path you had to cross to come to this very moment. Without all of those experiences, there would not be this present and this you. So, be thankful for each moment that you went through because all of them together brought you here, to today. Look at your past as a train which led you here to where you are now. It is nonsense to go over every scene you did not like during your journey time and time again. Choose precious memories from the trip to save and let go of everything you do not want to carry along any further.

How to Let Go?

Forgive. Practicing forgiveness will set you free. It is a precious gift, not for the one you forgive, but for yourself. When you experience negative emotions, you are the one who is producing them, not the person who hurt you. When you carry toxic feelings, you are the one who will be poisoned, not others. Forgiveness is the cure. If you do not know how to forgive and let go, in the beginning, it is enough just to be willing to do so. "I'm willing to forgive. I'm willing to let it go." Those the affirmations that could serve you in this case.

Visualize yourself and the person you want to forgive. Imagine yourself telling them, "I forgive you. I set you free. I set myself free." Imagine white, healing light shining on both of you. And then visualize that person going away from your life, free. Feel lighter and freer. Do the same for everyone who needs your forgiveness.

When you forgive everything and everyone who has ever treated you poorly, it is time to forgive yourself. Recall every possible thing you could need forgiveness for. Then imagine yourself covered with the white light. Hug yourself mentally and tell yourself, "I forgive you. Now you are free."

To clear all injustices and heal all the pain from the past, practice forgiveness often, on a daily basis. Forgive everything and everyone. Never carry that poison with yourself again.

Help Others

Nothing heals a soul better than helping others. If you are egocentric, your pain will be growing and tends to fill all spaces: all your attention, all your time, and all the energy you have. You should not ignore your emotions. Of course, you need to do everything you can to feel better and to heal your soul. But you should not let it become your only preoccupation. Do not let yourself become a slave to your own pain and the search for the cure. Why not try to move your focus for a change? You can shift your attention to some activity. Or even better, to help others. After helping others, you will feel better or may even find your purpose. This does not mean that you have to volunteer (even though that is an excellent way of serving). You can serve others by giving whatever you have: time, money, kindness, or service. It is enough to simply make someone a little happier or to do something nice for someone. If you make only one person's day, you will have done a great job.

Increase Awareness

Being aware means being mindful: knowing how to find your inner peace, listening to the voice of your soul, and being aware of everything inside of or around you.

You can increase your awareness by practicing the methods and techniques we have already discussed: introspection and meditation. In that way, you will become aware of your thoughts, feelings, beliefs, and patterns. And you will be able to change them. That is the point from which you can start improving your life and healing your soul. That would be absolutely impossible without awareness. By working on your self-growth, your awareness will increase. Then later you will be able to follow your intuition and precisely feel the energy and intentions of others.

Be Grateful

Gratefulness is the most powerful tool for raising our vibration. There is no such a thing as an ungrateful happy person. So, include this magnificent cure in your healing. When you wake up in the morning, do not rush to leap out of bed. Stay there for a while, in peace, and think about all the things you could be thankful for: for waking up, for being able to open your eyes, for the sleep and rest that you had, for a new day, for your bed, for your mattress, for your pillow, and so on. You can go even further and be thankful for many more things, from your health to your children to the house that you live in. The fact that you are alive means there is a lot to be thankful for.

Before you fall asleep, think again about how grateful you are and recall all of the blessings that you can remember. You can practice this whenever you want to during the day. It will definitely raise your vibration immediately. If you adopt this as a life approach, you will guarantee yourself overall happiness and your soul will heal itself faster.

HARD TIMES

How to Survive

There are some hard times in life we would rather skip, but they are also a natural part of our life journey. If you apply some of the advice from this book, it should make it a bit easier for you to go through those challenging times and to become even stronger. Practicing these techniques and adopting the habits of meditation, introspection, healthy living, and self-love will help you to heal your soul and to find balance in your life. It will improve the quality of your life and make you happier. Besides all of that, here is some additional advice on how to survive the hard times and to help yourself recover from them.

How to Survive Loneliness

Everybody needs to be alone from time to time. But when it is too often or for a long time, we begin to feel lonely. Being alone is not bad. Being alone is not the same as feeling lonely. You can feel that way even if you are surrounded by people.

We are social beings. But can you tell why you feel so bad when you are alone? Do you think that you are not good enough if you have no company? Or you are bored? Whatever it is, remember that you are good company for yourself. You can have fun even without anyone else around. It is the right time for you to learn how to enjoy solitude, in silence, or to join a large group and feel like a part of a bigger community. Try to notice all of the benefits from being alone: you have plenty of time for yourself and for your self-growth, learning, hobbies, and passions. You are free to make your own decisions. It is also

41

the perfect time to learn how to be responsible and to make the right choices and decisions. Being in a healthy and happy relationship demands that you first know how to be happy alone. Loving someone requires you to first know how to love yourself. Instead of being sad or lonely, get the best out of this period in your life and use it wisely to build a great relationship with yourself and to grow as a person as much as you can. Do not think of it as permanent. It is just a phase. When you are ready, you can reach out for people.

How to Survive the End of a Relationship

The end of something can be really painful. It is perfectly natural to feel disappointment, sadness, and a whole spectrum of other emotions when a relationship comes to an end. But when all of it passes, you will be stronger and richer for having had that experience. It may sound cruel to say while you are still attached to your ex-love, but it is always better to end a relationship than stay in a dysfunctional one. Even though your partner is not supposed to make you happy all the time, the main point of being together is to share good and bad, to support and love each other. If you cannot get what you need out of a relationship, it can be more functional to move on alone. That is the reasonable, unromantic part of the story. And it can be useful, too, to shift the focus from your emotions.

When it is about feelings, do not try to avoid them just because they seem unbearable. Accept all of your emotions, feel them, and survive them. Only then will you be able to begin the process of healing your aching heart.

How to Survive the Loss of Loved Ones

There is no cure except time. Again, accept your feelings. Do not try to skip over the grief of a loss. Let yourself be sad. Let yourself cry. And give yourself time. Do not rush through healing because that would be unnatural and useless. In this case, time is working for you.

When you are ready, start to think about gratefulness. Of course, you cannot be thankful for your loss, but you can recall all of the good moments you had together and feel grateful for knowing that person and having had them in your life. Mentally hug that loved one, say goodbye, and let them go.

How to Survive Stressful Situations

When you find yourself in the middle of an emotional storm, the most important thing is to stay calm. Do not let the atmosphere carry you and try to resist the impulse to react. Act from your inner space instead. It is always a good idea to count to ten before you say something you could regret. Be wise and try to see the broader picture. Think not only about what is happening right in front of you but about the consequences and effects that it could have. Consider the motives of everyone involved and take into account their intentions. Thinking about all of these factors first will prevent you from acting impulsively.

If you get stressed, do not let it accumulate within you. Find a way to release stress on a daily basis so that it does not harm your inner peace and health.

CONCLUSION

Now you know everything you need to get back in touch with your deepest self, to hear the voice of your soul, and to follow the path of your heart.

What you do next will depend on many factors: where you are right now on the scale of your personal growth, if you are ready and willing to put some effort into finding peace, and what you want and expect from your life.

You know what is best and what path you should follow. This book is here to help you discover that information again. All of the answers are already there, within you.

This book, like all books in the world, has the intention of making you look deep inside yourself and reconnect with your soul on a deeper level. When you find peace and joy there, you will bring them to all fields of your life.

And this friend will be here for you, making you more confident with every reading.

NOTES

NOTES

Made in the USA
Middletown, DE
31 January 2020